EAST

MOUNTAINS

A 1940s Boyhood in the Rural Pacific Northwest

By Kingsley Woodhead

Preface

We are all products of our life experiences, especially those of childhood. For those who were born at a later time and grew up in urbanized environments, this tale reflects a different America and a different world than they have known. It is based on, and true to the essence of, actual life experiences. The people names are changed but the geographic names are actual.

Table of Contents

Moving East of the Mountains

One of my oldest and happiest memories is of the big old "Girl Scout House" on Mercer Island, where I lived with my mother and older sister, Ellen, when I was four and five years old. It was called the Girl Scout House because it had been willed to that organization by the old lady who had owned it and lived there for several decades. It was a potentially valuable property, a few forested acres on the shore of Lake Washington, but the Girl Scouts didn't have the funds available at that time to create a summer camp, as specified in the old lady's will, so they rented it out.

The house rented cheap because it was not in good condition, not having been kept up during the old lady's last years. It had been fairly elegant at one time, a tall Victorian with wide porches on three sides (ideal for playing on or under on rainy days). But it hadn't been painted in years and the once expansive gardens and yard had mostly been taken over by laurel and wild blackberry. The bathroom was no longer usable -- some problem with the septic tank -- so the tenants had to make do with an outhouse down a path through the blackberry vines and a big, galvanized wash tub brought into the kitchen from the back porch on bath nights. Gartersnakes among the blackberries sometimes added a little excitement to a trip down the privy path, especially for Ellen.

Looking back in later years, I realized the house had been an uncomfortable and unpleasant economic necessity to my mother. But I had thought it was wonderful.

Several boards had been removed from the land end of the little boat dock to keep me from playing on the dock and possibly going into the water, which was quite deep just a few feet from shore. It didn't take me long to discover the removed boards under a porch and begin using a couple as a catwalk to reach the dock.

Mercer Island 1942

Ellen was charged with keeping an eye on me during the two hours between the time I got home from kindergarten and she from school and when our mother returned from work at the sewing shop. I felt lucky that Ellen was usually more interested in late afternoon soap operas on the radio than in what I was up to outside. I quickly put the boards back under the porch when I heard my mother's Model A Ford chugging and popping down the long driveway from the road.

It was wartime and the Boeing aircraft plant at the South end of the lake was building planes for the war, including large seaplanes for the Navy. From time to time I would hear the distant growl of seaplane engines and rush to the end of the dock to stare joyfully as a big flying boat lumbered into view beyond the headland and lifted majestically into the air. I would wave vigorously as I imagined the plane and its heroic crew were on the way to bomb a menacing Japanese fleet off the coast.

I was fascinated by all things military, and especially the large number of men in uniform on the streets of Seattle.

Military uniforms for children were quite popular and it was not unusual to see peewee-sized soldiers, sailors and Marines. There were even WAC and WAVE uniforms for little girls. One of the best days of my life at that time was when my mother came home with a little blue sailor suit she had made for me. I would have worn it every day if my mother had permitted.

A couple of times during a trip across the floating bridge at night the air raid sirens began to wail and all the cars came to a stop and turned off their headlights and engines. The bridge lights also would flicker out. I excitedly rolled down the car window and stuck my head out into the silent darkness. Being careful not to make any noise that might betray the location of the bridge to a Japanese bomber crew listening overhead, I waited for the shrill whine of falling bombs as I had heard them in a newsreel at the movies. My mother told me repeatedly the air raids were just practice, not real, but I was sure there would be a real one sometime. I felt both relief and disappointment when the "all clear" sounded, lights came back on and engines churned to life.

Life in the Girl Scout house changed one day when my stepfather came home from the Army. Drafted in late 1942, at the age of 44, Mack Sawyer had entered the Army as a strapping, healthy construction worker -- the Army badly needed combat engineers. He was discharged a few months later as a weakened version of the man he had been.

First, he was one of the thousands of soldiers struck down by an influenza epidemic while they were crowded into makeshift wartime camps with poor sanitation. Second, he was one of the unlucky ones who couldn't tolerate sulfa drugs, the wonder medicine of that time that Army doctors dispensed wholesale. When it became obvious that soldiers like Mack Sawyer would need months to recover a reasonable level of health and strength, the Army gave them discharge papers and train tickets home. They didn't receive disability payments but did have veteran's preference for jobs in war industries, when they became physically able to work.

Mack Sawyer was not ready to do physical labor when he first got home. He slept a lot and Ellen and I were instructed by our mother not to make noise or do anything to disturb or annoy the gaunt figure who seemed to me more like a ghost than a man. And an ill-tempered ghost. The weatherbeaten old house on Mercer Island was not as happy or as much fun anymore.

After a few weeks our stepfather, although not yet at full strength, took advantage of his veteran's preference to claim a job at a shipyard across the lake. What he didn't tell his bosses was that he was only going to work there long enough to save up sufficient money to move East of the mountains, back to the rural "dry side" of the state. He'd grown up and lived all his life there, except for a couple of years trying his luck in California, until the Depression drove him over to "the coast" in search of work. Although it provided him a badly needed job and a new wife (his second), the West side of the state never earned his gratitude or became home to him. Soon after he left the Army his brother Frank, foreman of a large orchard up the

Okanogan River, near Canada, had written to offer him a job.

Persons employed in critical war industries were not free to quit their jobs without official permission. Nevertheless, Mack Sawyer collected his pay envelope on a Friday and by the time his shift began Monday morning he was 250 miles away (by road) on the East side of the Cascade Mountains that divide Washington state from North to South. As he had suspected, he never heard from any official source about his unauthorized departure from the shipyard.

On a dreary, drizzly December Saturday, Mack and Lilly Sawyer loaded up the newly-purchased 1938 Lafayette coupe with their kids and as much of their household goods as could be stuffed into the trunk (which was so full the lid couldn't close and had to be tied) or tied onto the roof, and left the Girl Scout house and the island forever. Such of their goods as could not be squeezed into or onto the little car were abandoned.

The Lafayette had had a couple of nearly bald tires that were not likely to hold up all the way over the mountains, especially with the car so overloaded. New tires were not available to ordinary folks, who had to make do with retreads (used tires with some new rubber bonded onto them). But Mack Sawyer was determined to get two new tires, figuring the country owed him that much for what the Army had done to him. At the Sears store he asked to see the manager and explained his situation. He said if he didn't get away from the wet winter weather he might not survive until Spring.

Surprisingly, the manager was sufficiently moved to sell Mack two new tires, in violation of Federal rationing rules. And he didn't make him go around to the back of the store to pick up the tires unseen. Mack carried them through the store, one hanging from each arm, ignoring the looks of envy and resentment on the faces of other shoppers, his face set in an expression of stony defiance that I would come to know well over the years.

Since the coupe had no rear seat, I rode lying on the wide ledge between the seat backs and the rear window. Ellen squeezed in beside her mother. Luckily, she was skinny enough to fit.

The trip across the mountains was the best adventure I had ever experienced. As the Lafayette labored up the Stevens Pass highway, snow appeared on the sides of the road. The snow got deeper as we climbed until we were driving in a trench with white walls as high as the car. Nothing could be seen out the car windows except the black- green-white stands of trees that towered above the snow walls. As darkness fell, the trees melted into an almost tangible blackness and only the road ahead could be seen, for a short distance, the white walls and compacted snow on the roadway glistening in the car's headlights.

I turned my head and looked out the rear window into total emptiness, savoring a tingling sensation that all the world had disintegrated except for the hundred feet or so of snowy highway ahead. As sleep overtook me, I watched white flakes begin to attach themselves to the window and listened to the rhythmic swipes of the windshield wipers.

I awoke with a start, something was wrong. There was no sound of the car's engine, no crunch of the tires on the snow-packed road, no swoosh of windshield wipers. I jerked my head around but could see nothing inside the car. A tiny surge of panic rose in my groin and wiggled upward. My heart increased its tempo. Just as fear was about to take hold, my mother's soft voice floated in the blackness. "Are you awake?"

I took a deep breath and said, "Yeah."

"Well, go back to sleep. We're going to be here until it gets light. Are you warm enough?"

I said I was and laid my head back down, but sleep had been frightened away and was slow to return. Before I sank back down I was comforted to hear the soft snoring of my stepfather and the slow, even breathing of my mother. Their heads were only inches away but it was only by sound that I was reassured of that. I couldn't see anything. I had never before experienced such a total, lonely darkness.

When I next awoke, I was happy to see that it was getting light out and I could see dimly the interior of the car. The starter growled for several seconds and finally the engine coughed and came to life. My stepfather opened his door, which required a deal of pushing because snow had drifted up around the car. Only then did I notice that nothing was visible through the windows. All were frosted with snow, allowing a little light in but no vision out.

When my stepfather exited, I quickly slid down onto the seat and followed him out. I took a deep breath of the delicious, crisp mountain air. Except for the open driver's side door, the car was almost hidden inside a snow drift. My stepfather had pulled off the road into a service station lot. Snow was drifted up around the door and windows of the building and the gas pumps were white pillars.

I gazed in wonder at my surroundings. I had never seen so much snow or even imagined it was possible.

The whole world was buried under a whipped cream coating. As I moved around the car to help my stepfather retrieve it from the snow I had to plow through powder as high as my waist. I was exhilarated. It was even better when my mother told me we were at the summit, above 4,000 feet.

By the time we had all taken our turns going behind the service station building to relieve ourselves, the engine was warm and we pulled back onto the highway. To complaints of hunger from Ellen and me, our mother assured us there was a truck stop that would be open a few miles down the road. Our empty stomachs grew impatient as the few miles stretched into quite a few but we knew it would be better to suffer in silence. As the sun rose higher, the snowy terrain became blindingly, almost painfully, white.

With breakfast inside us, we rode on, mile after mile. As we descended from the mountains to the foothills and valleys below, the snow wasn't as deep anymore but it still covered almost everything in all directions. Just before the small city of Wenatchee we turned

North for the 120-mile drive, first along the Columbia River and then, at Brewster, tracing the Okanogan River upstream toward Canada.

I watched the snowy landscape roll away behind the car with feelings both of fascination and alienation. It was utterly different from the countryside I was accustomed to. There were scattered clusters of smallish evergreen trees on the slopes of the mountains flanking the river valley. I was used to looking out at hills and the mountains beyond that were covered with almost unbroken forest. I had always lived in a green world and this one was brown, tan or gray wherever the land showed through the snow cover. And the mountains seemed to be as much rock as soil, punctuated with huge, steep outcroppings of mostly gray or almost white rock.

In a vague way that I didn't understand, I felt like an intruder in this land. The look of the landscape made me feel out of place and a little bit lonely. It seemed like a mostly empty country and it made a bit of an empty place inside me. In all the following years that I lived in Okanogan County and, later, the Columbia Basin, I never got much beyond an uneasy truce with the land East of the mountains.

The Orchard

The house provided by the orchard owners for Frank Sawyer, his wife Milly and their two sons was very impressive to me. It was roomy and modern, had central heating and a bathroom that could be used. We lived in Uncle Frank's house for a few weeks until a worker's cabin became available for us in the orchard's labor camp. The cabin was quite a comedown from the stepuncle's house, yet it was better than the workers' cabins on most of the orchards and ranches in the county, or in most counties.

On the Ellerby Orchard, at a few hundred acres one of the largest in the county, the workers' cabins were recently built of cement block construction. They were arranged in two facing rows with a large communal latrine and laundry room dividing the cabins into two sections. There were two rooms per cabin, with a block wall between, to house two workers or families in each cabin. Because of his brother, my stepfather was allowed to chop a doorway through the block center wall so we could occupy both rooms. Apple boxes, orange crates and nail kegs served as furniture for most of the inhabitants, including us. Only a few of the cabins were occupied year-round, as most of the workers were seasonal. The camp was bustling with people from late Spring until late Fall, almost deserted through the winter. Mack Sawyer was one of the few year-round workers.

Orchard Labor Camp 1944

A few yards behind the second row of cabins the land sloped down for 30 or 40 feet to a long, narrow pasture running along the Okanogan River.

During Spring high water most of the pasture was under a foot or so of water where the river was almost twice as wide as normal. As the river receded back within its banks, it left several small ponds that would shrink and disappear as Summer began. These ponds were an irresistable attraction for me and the other young boys from the labor camp. Of course, they were strictly off- limits, as likely deathtraps for unsupervised children. Since nearly all the adults did some kind of work around the orchard, children were unsupervised during at least part of each day.

The ponds provided sport in the hunting of frogs, turtles and many kinds of insects. But what I liked best was to tie a length of string to the end of a long stick, fix a fish hook fashioned from a safety pin, baited with a worm or grasshopper, and dangle it into the water. I never caught a fish from the river or the ponds but it was just as well, as I wouldn't have dared take my trophy home if I had caught something.

Fishing and baseball were my favorite forms of play but I had to teach myself how to do them. Although my stepfather was himself an avid angler and played baseball with other orchard workers on summer evenings, he had no interest in teaching me or providing me a fishing pole or baseball glove. Our stepfather's interest in Ellen and me was mostly limited to whether we did our chores without reminder, minded when told to do something, didn't talk back, didn't eat too much and generally weren't a bother. He didn't legally adopt us and never asked us to call him "Dad." We didn't. Many people thought we were ill-mannered to address our stepfather by his first name but I would rather have been sent to an orphanage than call that man "Dad" or take his last name.

Despite the threat of corporal punishment if I got caught, I found the river edge too tempting to stay away from. I even would roll up my trouser legs sometimes and wade out several feet. I never tired of feeling the mud ooze up between my toes as the river eddies worked to undercut my footing. One time I got careless and fell to my hands and knees, soaking my bib overalls and T-shirt. Luckily, it was a hot summer day and I could stay away from the cabin until my clothes had dried.

Another hot summer day introduced me to a new emotion -- hatred. I was exploring the river bank with a boy a few years older. I felt good that the older boy seemed to welcome my company and treated me almost as an equal.

We came across a turtle at the water's edge, the biggest turtle I had ever seen, the size of a small dinner plate. When I found turtles or frogs I was always careful not to injure them. I would hold them, look at them for a little while and then leave them to their business as I went on to see what else I might find.

The older boy had other ideas. He flipped the turtle onto its back and poked at it with a sharp stick as it flailed its legs trying to right itself. I told the boy to stop what he was doing and let the turtle go. The boy dismissed my entreaty with scorn. I tried to get hold of the turtle but was roughly knocked aside.

Worse was yet to come. After a few minutes the boy took a jackknife from his pocket and cut into the turtle's underside. Tears began to roll down my cheeks as the boy crudely hacked the turtle open and dug out its entrails. When he tired of this sport the boy threw the remains of the turtle as far out into the river as he could. As he walked away he cursed me as a stupid little crybaby. I passionately wished I were big enough and strong enough to give the boy a good thrashing. I cried all the way back to the cabin.

The pasture later provided me another unhappy memory. Among the several draft horses used on the orchard was a huge white stallion named Toby. Toby was very old and didn't move very fast but could still pull a wagon and be useful. But it was mostly sentiment that kept him on the place. The elder Mr. Ellerby had owned Toby for almost 20 years and would probably have kept him even if he were of no use at all. Toby was much loved by the children of the labor camp because the man in charge of the horses would sometimes give children a ride on Toby's back, so large it could accommodate three or four children at a time. A few of the older children were sometimes allowed to ride

Toby alone, with a warning not to make him run faster than a slow trot.

A year after we moved into the labor camp, the Spring high water flooded the pasture, as usual, and left its residual ponds. The horses were not let into the pasture until it had dried out. But somehow, early one morning, Toby got through the fence and down into the still boggy pasture, lured by the lush new growth of grass. At the edge of a pond his great weight drove his forehooves deeply into the mud. As he struggled to free himself he just sank deeper. By the time somebody noticed his plight he was thoroughly exhausted.

A crew of men and a tractor were hurried to his aid. They struggled for some time to free him from the stubborn grip of the mud, a task made difficult by Toby's massive bulk and weight. By the time they finally got him free his heart had been taxed beyond survival. Ellen and I and other children, watching from the higher ground behind the cabins, mourned his passing with copious tears.

Several months before Toby's misfortune, my first Summer at the orchard eased toward Fall and right after Labor Day the school year began. The children from the orchard labor camp, along with some from several farms and orchards within a few miles, were among the last in the state to attend an old-style one-room school. Grades one through six totalled about 20 students after the many children of seasonal workers had departed for work elsewhere. Junior high and high school students had a long bus ride into the town of Tonasket, about a dozen miles to the South.

The one-room Ellisford school was about a half-mile from the labor camp. At the South edge of the Ellerby land a road crossed the river on an old, narrow wooden bridge, linking the roads that followed each side of the river. The school was just South of the bridge road, on a low bluff beside the river. Where the bridge road met the road along the East side of the river, a short distance from the school, were a gas station and small grocery store. These were the entire business district of the hamlet of Ellisford, not counting the school and a church a short distance to the South.

On the first day of school Ellen and I walked together down the highway to the gas station and then along a dirt driveway to the school. I was beginning first grade and Ellen the sixth. The school was full to overflowing with students the first few weeks, making things a little chaotic. After apple harvest, the seasonal families departed for California farms and the tiny student body stabilized for the winter.

For some reason, the teacher, Mrs. Packer, quickly took a liking to me and went out of her way to help and encourage me. Perhaps it was because, unlike many of the other boys, and even some of the girls, I really liked school and took to reading very easily. She was a patient person and a teacher of many years experience but probably concluded fairly quickly whether a new student showed scholarly promise or was unlikely to achieve much more than rudimentary reading, writing and arithmetic skills. She seemed to ration her time and attention on that basis and I benefited.

Frank Sawyer's two sons also attended Ellisford school and I soon built a friendship with the younger son, Kyle, just a few months older than me and also a first grader. I hadn't been able to do that when we lived in the stepuncle's house the previous Winter. The older son, Frankie, had been an impediment to our friendship at that time because he was a bully by nature and enjoyed tormenting us and instigating fights between us. At school, Frankie's attention shifted to other boys his own age, leaving Kyle and me in peace, mostly.

Kyle was at home in the rural environment, having lived most of his life, and all of it he could remember, on the orchard property. He gave me some useful information, such as where to watch out for poisonous black widow spiders and the exotic fun of eating chokecherries. There were two small chokecherry trees behind the school and some of the younger boys climbed in their branches each recess, while the fruit lasted. The chief attraction of chokecherries was not the taste but the purple fuzz that collected on the teeth and the roof of the mouth when they were eaten. When the boys returned to the schoolroom, in response to Mrs.

Packer ringing her handbell, their lips and tongues were purple and they could spend a few minutes back at their desks amusing themselves with the process of licking away the fuzz inside their mouths.

The best part of school for me, however, was school. Being in the same room when the fourth, fifth and sixth graders were reading aloud or getting instruction from Mrs. Packer, the first and second grade students were exposed to more kinds of information than they would have been in a classroom of their own. Exposure to the elixir of learning stimulated my curiosity about almost everything -- everything except arithmetic. I didn't much like arithmetic unless it was wrapped in facts about animals or volcanoes or geography. I was especially fond of geography. There were so many places previously unknown to me, places utterly different from anything I had known about -- deserts, jungles, savannah, polar regions, tropical islands. Besides other places, I was fascinated by other times -- ancient Rome or Egypt, or the time of dinosaurs or cavemen or knights on horseback. Kyle and I and some of the other boys at recess killed dinosaurs by the dozen, armed with imaginary stone axes and spears and plenty of loud grunting in caveman talk.

The railroad was another popular feature of attendance at the little school. The tracks ran parallel to the road and between the gas station and the school. Except during apple harvest there were only one or two trains a week going North or South. But when the packing sheds were shipping thousands of boxes of apples, the train ran every day, sometimes twice a day. The children got to know the days and times the train would go by and never tired of lining up along the edge of the school yard to wave and shout. The engineer and fireman would smile and wave back and sometimes the engineer would loudly release some steam that would envelop the children like fog.

A favorite sport, though we were repeatedly admonished not to do it, was to place one or two coins -- usually pennies -- on the steel rails before the train came by. After the train passed there was a scramble to find the flattened coins among the gravel of the roadbed. Almost every student had at least one squashed coin as a lucky charm. To me, the two mashed pennies in my pocket were a link to the train and, thus, to everywhere the train might go, even across the country to exotic places like Chicago or New York. After the first few days of school, Ellen and I joined the other students from the orchard labor camp walking to and from school along the railroad tracks, instead of on the road.

Walking on the railroad tracks often made me think about ideas that had come to me in school. Mrs. Packer was teaching the older students about the great ice age. She said if we had been inside the school 15,000 years earlier, we would have been squashed flat under a mile of ice. And she told them that a few million years before that, we would have been at the bottom of a great sea.

I thought about those things a lot after that. As I balanced myself walking along the thin steel rail I would picture the wheels of the train rolling over the very place where I was. I'd reach into my pocket and feel the two pennies, squeezed out to half again their normal size by the weight of that monstrous black locomotive. I didn't quite understand it, but I sensed that existence was linked to where time and position intersect. If one was at a certain place at a certain time, it could change everything.

There were other ideas I became aware of during the year we lived on the orchard. An important one was that there were some people who were to be avoided, as far as having social contact. If these people had children, I was not to play with those children. I was not to go into their cabins or accept a cookie or piece of candy if offered by their mothers. And I was forbidden to ever bring those children around our cabin. This was my stepfather's idea. The people to be shunned spoke a little differently than people who were "okay" and they came from places with names like Oklahoma or Arkansas or South Carolina. At first, I had good intentions of not playing with those children. But over time, especially as I shared a schoolroom and schoolyard with them, I often forgot my good intentions. But I never fell so far from grace as to go to their cabins or bring them to mine.

Another idea that I discovered that year on the orchard was that grown men like to drink stuff called whiskey and beer. I would see a small group of men standing around at the spray house and one would pull a small bottle out of his overalls, take a drink and pass the bottle around for the others to drink from. They'd do the same with pouches of chewing tobacco or cans of "snoose."

The spray house was where they mixed the poison spray in big vats and pumped it into tractor-towed sprayers. It was sprayed onto the fruit trees to kill the various pests that could damage the fruit. I heard some people say they thought the use of those sprays had something to do with the high rate of cancer locally.

Our stepfather seemed always to have his own bottle of whiskey at the cabin. He usually didn't drink from it during the week but would partake liberally between Friday evening and Sunday afternoon. Ellen and I knew to stay clear of him on weekends as much as possible. Our mother told us he drank because he still had pain from a back injury suffered when he worked on Grand Coulee Dam several years before. But the whiskey didn't seem to make him any happier or friendlier, at least toward us.

The Log Cabin

In the Spring of 1945 Mack and Lilly put a down payment on a parcel of land beside the Okanogan River, a few miles North of Tonasket. It included a small log house that immediately became the "Log Cabin" in the family roster of residences.

The Log Cabin 1946

Besides the log house, there was a truck-sized garage with a loft, a lean-to woodshed beside the garage and a small barn and chicken coop at the back of the property, where the land sloped down to the river. We were back to using an outhouse, behind the garage, but acquired some real furniture from Mack's friend Irv Green, who owned a second-hand store in Tonasket. Ellen and I still slept on Army surplus camp cots but at least in a separate room from our mother and stepfather.

The kitchen was a relic from an earlier time. At the sink, instead of a faucet, there was a hand pump to draw water in from the cistern behind the house. The cistern had to be refilled from time to time with water from the irrigation flume. Since flume water was not free of contaminants, it had to be filtered through several inches of sand before entering the cistern. It was a primitive system but it worked. At least nobody contracted a disease or parasite.

A galvanized wash tub on the back porch, along with a knuckle-buster washboard and water heated on the kitchen stove, was how laundry got done. The tub was brought into the kitchen on bath nights. Our mother and Ellen and I bathed on Friday evenings and our stepfather on Saturday evenings. My mother and Ellen got the bath water before me so it was already somewhat murky with soap residue when I got in, but some fresh hot water had been added.

I was happy to make the move but soon discovered my share of daily chores would demand a lot of my time and energy. At first there was just the garden to weed, mullein plants to be dug out of the pasture and wood chopped by our stepfather to be carried in to the woodbox by the kitchen stove. The woodbox had to be full anytime my stepfather checked on it. It seemed my stepfather found other things for me to do if he saw me playing or idling. I became adept at staying out of his line of sight.

In the Fall there was butchering to be done, another new experience for Ellen and me. We had assigned duties for this project, too. As our stepfather chopped the head off each chicken, he placed the headless bird into a gunny sack to limit its thrashing around and possibly bruising the meat. As each sack quit moving, I pulled out the chicken and placed it into a large steel drum resting on bricks, with a wood fire burning underneath to keep the water hot.

Our mother extracted the birds one at a time from the hot water and, with Ellen's help, plucked off the feathers and pin feathers. This work was done on a makeshift table of boards resting on a pair of sawhorses. When the last chicken had been decapitated, everyone joined in to finish the plucking. When all the birds were naked, our mother and stepfather began gutting them, carefully saving the giblets and depositing the rest into a wash tub to later become fertilizer. Once cleaned and drawn, the chickens went into the kitchen to be cut up and wrapped in waxed paper. By late afternoon they had been taken into town and deposited in the rented freeze locker at the creamery.

Ellen and I didn't have to help with the butchering and skinning of the rabbits as it required some skill and experience. But when my stepfather decided to give up on raising rabbits, I was tasked, despite, or perhaps because of, my vigorous protest, to dispose of some unwanted baby rabbits. I wasn't given a clue how to go about it and botched the nasty business badly, causing the bunnies more painful deaths than I had wanted to. I didn't soon forgive myself or my stepfather.

The following Spring, we added ducks and a few geese to the livestock inventory. Our stepfather warned Ellen and me not to make pets of the ducks because they were to be butchered in the Fall. It was easy for us to resist making pets of chickens, and the geese weren't interested in being friends, but it was different with the ducks. In spite of our stepfather's warning, we each became attached to a couple of the ducks and spent extra time hand feeding and petting them. When one of us showed up at the duck pen the chosen pets would rush forward, looking for a handout. It was a dark day for Ellen and me when all the ducks met their preordained fate.

A milk cow, a hereford calf and some piglets were also bought that Spring. With money limited, Mack Sawyer did carpentry work in exchange for most of the new livestock. The piglets presented a challenge because they proved adept at wriggling through or under the fence of the new pig pen and scampering down the road a quarter-mile or so to the Lutz's place where they were born. After their second breakout Herm Lutz was becoming annoyed but the pig pen was finally made escape-proof. "Slopping" the pigs and feeding the calf were added to my daily chores. The jersey cow, an expensive investment, received its care, including milking, from our stepfather.

Both Mack and Lilly worked away from home during all but the mid-Winter days. With so much unsupervised time, and so many assigned chores that were supposed to be completed before our mother and stepfather got home from work, about 6 p.m., it was almost inevitable that my performance of duties would most days be found unsatisfactory by my stepfather and punishable. Mack Sawyer had been raised on a homestead at Alta Lake by a father whose guiding principle was, "Spare the rod and spoil the child." He spoiled none of his children and Mack carried on his tradition.

In the Spring of 1947 Mack and Lilly began building a new house on the property, with the intention of moving into it as soon as they got the roof on and the windows installed and then finishing it while living in it. Built of pumice blocks, this was the "Block House." As soon as we moved the couple hundred feet to the block house they divided the property into two parcels and sold the half with the log house and barn. The block house was finished by Fall and we once more enjoyed the luxury of an indoor bathroom and the new luxuries of an electric kitchen stove and a refrigerator, instead of an icebox. But such gracious living was of brief duration. By the following Spring the block house had been sold to finance the purchase of several acres from Tom Dolan, a couple miles closer to town. For a few months we rented an apartment in the Whitestone Hotel in town and our mother operated a sewing shop in a room facing the street. I got permission to utilize the shoeshine stand in the hotel lobby that had been unused for a long time and was able to make a little bit of pocket money, my first earnings.

The Block House 1947

Mrs. Hoffman & Annalee Haney

I usually enjoyed a good relationship with my teachers and that was true with Mrs. Hoffman in the fourth grade -- until the final weeks of the school year.

The fourth grade class occupied a room in the daylight basement part of the school building. The window sills inside the room were at about eye level of the tallest students. Outside, the windows were only a few inches above the ground. In the warm weather of late Spring the windows were open and at recess or noon hour some boys would climb through a window to go in or out instead of using the basement door. This was prohibited and Mrs. Hoffman had sent two or three boys to the principal's office that Spring and given the class a stern lecture on the subject. She was a stickler for the rules.

One day at recess, I was on my hands and knees outside a window, talking to a boy inside the classroom. Mrs. Hoffman, who was writing some lesson information on the blackboard, turned and saw me at the window. She gave me a look that said, "Don't even think about climbing through that window," and turned back to the blackboard. I intended to come back inside but I had not intended to come in through the window. I got up and ran to the basement door and down the short hall to the classroom. I was standing near the window when Mrs. Hoffman turned again, saw me and thought I had climbed through the window. Her cheeks flushed red and her face took on a fierce expression. In a loud, icy voice she said, "Come here." As I approached her she said, "What have you been told about climbing through the window?" When I quickly responded, "I didn't," her face flushed a deeper red and her fist shot out, striking me squarely in the chest. I staggered backward and before I could say anything more she ordered, "Get to your desk." As tears began to well up, I walked to my desk, aware that I was being watched by all the other students.

For the rest of that day I didn't absorb any lesson information because my mind was fully occupied with a burning resentment. I thought about asking some of my classmates who saw me come in through the door to tell Mrs. Hoffman. But in the end I decided to just nurse my feelings of victimization and injustice. I didn't raise my hand or take part in any classroom discussions during the last two weeks of school. Mrs. Hoffman made a token effort at reconciliation but I refused to respond.

This had not been the only time I had been punished unfairly but it stung the most and remained fresh in my mind the longest. Yet, somehow, over time, I began to connect the incident with the shameful treatment of classmate Annalee Haney, in which I had been a participant a few times.

Annalee Haney was what at that time was called mildly retarded. She also was rather homely, wore thick glasses and often laughed when nothing was funny. The teachers and some of the girl students tried to shield Annalee as best they could but some teasing and tormenting went on anyway. It took some time for me to come to regret my participation in making life at school unpleasant for Annalee Haney.

Somewhere in my later musings, the thought came to me that maybe I did deserve the chastisement by Mrs. Hoffman, not for what she mistakenly thought I had done, but for being mean to Annalee, for which I had never been punished.

Having a visually-oriented imagination, I envisioned a ledger book somewhere in which a person's incidents of bad behavior were recorded. I found some comfort in the fanciful notion that maybe bad luck or injustices suffered, along with any acts of kindness, might be entered in the ledger to offset my moral debits. My long-term regret was that I would not have the opportunity to apologize in person to Annalee. My hope was that, in the end, my ledger account would have more entries in the credit column than the debit column.

Charlie Tall Bear

One of the new students in my fifth grade class when the new school year began in September 1948 was a husky Indian boy named Dennis Wolfe. He was taller and heavier than all but a couple of the other fifth grade boys and was probably the strongest. He definitely was the meanest, perhaps as a defense mechanism in what he perceived as a hostile white man's world. He soon intimidated most of his classmates, which increased the level of unspoken hostility toward him and his sense of alienation.

Dennis Wolfe was notably unenthusiastic about learning white man's history, white man's arithmetic or white man's language. But the teacher, Miss Lloyd, was not one who would readily accept being stymied by a recalcitrant student.

A short, rotund woman of early middle age, Miss Lloyd was nonetheless surprisingly fleet afoot, able to move quickly to any desk in the room to chastise a boy gazing out the windows daydreaming or otherwise misbehaving. This chastisement often involved a loud smack on the head with the wooden ruler she nearly always had in her hand. She apparently bought several new rulers each year as sometimes they broke on contact. I had nearly been caught a time or two but on the whole had arrived at an amiable relationship with Miss Lloyd. She tolerated a certain amount of smartaleckiness from me because I was a good student.

A test of wills soon developed between the indifferent Indian boy and the determined teacher. Over a few weeks, Miss Lloyd began to wear him down. His desultory responses to questions and mumbling recitations of text passages gave her at least a partial victory. He was participating, however reluctantly.

A few days after school resumed from apple harvest break, Miss Lloyd conducted an oral quiz on a couple of chapters in the geography textbook that she'd assigned for reading during the break. When she called on Dennis Wolfe he gave an absurdly wrong answer. I laughed loudly and most of the class joined in. Miss Lloyd slammed the ruler down on her desk and commanded, "Quiet!" The expression on her face brought silence and chased the smiles from students' faces. After a few seconds of electric silence, she began in a quiet, icy voice, "Not one of you in this class is so smart that you have any right to laugh at anyone else's mistakes."

As she continued to scold, she turned her scowl toward every student, but looked at me longer than at anyone else, a fact I didn't fail to notice. My ears burned. I also didn't fail to notice that Dennis Wolfe fixed me with a long stare. Many had laughed. But I had laughed first.

After the students had eaten at their desks the sandwiches brought from home, washed down with mugs of milk supplied by the school, they were free to go outside for the rest of the noon hour.

As I walked through the outside door, headed for the playfield, something struck the back of my head, knocking me off balance so that I almost fell to the sidewalk. Stunned and bewildered, I caught my balance and whirled around to see where the blow had come from. Dennis Wolfe stood beside the door, his face set in an angry glower. Before I could quite grasp what was happening, my attacker struck again, the heel of his hand smacking into my forehead, knocking me back several steps. As I tried to clear my head, my attacker growled, "Why aren't ya laughin' ? C'mon, let's hear ya laugh now, white boy."

Dennis then quickly moved past me and walked toward the playfield. A few seconds later a teacher came out the door. Dennis Wolfe had apparently seen her coming toward the door. The teacher gave me a strange look but didn't stop or speak. I hoped the teacher had seen what happened but she gave no indication that she had.

I stood there a minute or two, trying to decide whether to go on to the playfield or go back inside. I decided I wasn't going to give Dennis Wolfe the satisfaction of chasing me to the safety of the classroom. I figured Dennis Wolfe had gotten his revenge and that should be the end of it. I figured wrong. My season of misery had just begun.

Over the following weeks Dennis Wolfe made life very unpleasant for me, waylaying me both inside and outside the school with hits, slaps, kicks and tripping. To make things worse, most of my classmates were aware of my plight and that I was powerless to fight back against my much bigger and stronger tormentor. Also adding to my distress was Georgie Bach, who attached himself to Dennis as a kind of toady sidekick, keeping tabs on my whereabouts to report to Dennis. At every opportunity, Georgie supplied verbal abuse to accompany the physical assaults. My hopes that some teacher would become aware of the situation and act went unfulfilled. For the first time ever, I hated coming to school.

As the Winter Solstice approached, darkness and cold claimed more and more of each day, an appropriate background for what my life had become. But before the shortest, darkest day of the year arrived, I found a personal sunbeam to brighten and warm my existence. The sunbeam was named Charlie Talber.

One morning, as students filed into their classrooms, the fifth graders noticed a stranger in their room. He didn't look like he belonged in fifth grade, he looked like he belonged in junior high. When I entered the room I saw Miss Lloyd beckon me to her desk. She motioned for me to come close as she swiveled her chair around to turn her back to the class. I was a little nervous, wondering if I was in some kind of trouble -- another burden piled onto my aching back. But Miss Lloyd was not handing me trouble. She was throwing me a life preserver.

In a very quiet voice she told me that the new student, an Indian boy named Charlie Talber, was joining the class and she was going to sit him in the desk next to me. She explained that Charlie should have been in the seventh grade but he had missed so much school that he was barely at fifth grade level. He lived with his uncle, who was a ranch hand and rodeo rider. His uncle's occupation caused him to move around a lot and that meant frequently pulling Charlie out of school to go on the road from one rodeo to another.

Getting to the meat of the matter, Miss Lloyd said she wanted me to help Charlie as much as I could so that Charlie could keep up with the class and not get discouraged and quit trying. I felt a warm glow of appreciation for the confidence Miss Lloyd seemed to have in me. Only much later did it occur to me that she might have purposely acted to solve two problems -- Charlie's, and mine.

She waved me to my seat and summoned Charlie to her desk. After a couple minutes of hushed conversation, Charlie looked toward me and then moved to the desk beside mine, already vacated by another student. I smiled and put out my hand. The Indian boy took my hand and shook it gingerly. His hand was much larger than mine and was well calloused. I sensed that Charlie could have squeezed my hand hard enough to bring me to my knees in pain, if he had wanted to.

For the first hour or two I divided my attention between my own work and helping Charlie. After a while Charlie seemed to relax a little and became more responsive. By noon we had formed the basis for a friendship. I was careful not to repeat my mistake of laughing at what might seem to me to be foolish mistakes.

When the students lined up to receive their hot cocoa, Charlie took his mug and went over to the window and stood looking out. I saw that he wasn't eating anything, apparently not having brought a lunch to school. I went to the window and stood beside Charlie and said softly, "Hey, you want half my sandwich?"

Charlie shook his head and mumbled, "No, that's okay. I'm not very hungry."

I held out the sandwich half. It was a particularly good one this day, meatloaf on my mother's homemade whole wheat bread. "C'mon, I got plenty, take it."

The boy looked down at the sandwich and then at me. I was trying to give him a look of encouragement. Charlie smiled faintly and took the sandwich with a whispered, "Thanks."

When we'd finished the sandwich and some cookies -- Charlie would only accept one -- and drunk our cocoa, Charlie said, "Let's go outside a while."

On the playfield, several boys were having a snowball fight and Charlie and I stood watching. Suddenly, a snowball that had been squeezed and compacted until it was really an iceball smashed into the side of my head, stinging my ear so much that I reflexively felt to see if it was bleeding. Even before I turned to look I knew who had launched the missile. Georgie Bach's squeals of laughter confirmed it. It hurt a lot but it was the last attack I would have to suffer at the hands of Dennis Wolfe.

As I brushed away the icy clumps from my hair and down my collar, Charlie asked, "Why did he smack you?"

"He hates me. He always picks on me."

"How come?"

I hesitated and then decided to tell the truth, "Because I laughed at him once."

Charlie gazed at Dennis, packing another iceball as he sneered at me. "Let's go talk to him," Charlie said and walked toward Dennis. I followed a few paces behind.

"I don't want you pickin' on Curtis anymore."

Dennis Wolfe turned his head and spit. "What's it to you?"

"He's my friend. So leave him alone."

"Why in hell you stickin' up for a white boy? He's a turd!"

"I told you, he's my friend."

Dennis Wolfe sized Charlie up for several seconds. The older boy was half a head taller and many pounds heavier, plus he gave the impression of being very strong. But Dennis wasn't convinced. He started to spout a string of curse words but at about the third word Charlie's hand shot out, grabbed Dennis's wrist and shoved the hand holding the iceball upward, smashing it into its maker's face so hard that Dennis stumbled backward. Clumps of icy snow had gone up into his nostrils and into his mouth. He sputtered and shook his head, snorted and spit to clear the snow from his nose and mouth.

Charlie moved up against him and said in a low, menacing voice, "You wanna pick on somebody, from now on you pick on me. Got it?"

Dennis Wolfe glared up at Charlie's eyes for several seconds, wanting to retaliate. But, as boys liked to say, just two things were holding him back -- fear and common sense. He turned away and walked slowly across the playfield. Georgie Bach stood unmoving for a few beats, looking unsure whether he should trot after his fallen idol. He apparently decided being buddies with the second toughest kid in fifth grade was better than nothing and followed Dennis across the playfield.

From that day, I once again enjoyed coming to school. And as the weeks passed I came to appreciate Charlie for much more than protection. Although

Charlie was lacking in book knowledge for a 12-year-old, he was far more learned in other matters than almost any boy his age, or even older boys.

I was greatly impressed to discover that Charlie knew all about horses and cattle, he was as at home in the saddle as on his feet. He knew how to repair harness, saddles and bridles. He had been driving his uncle's pickup since he was nine, in addition to tractors. He not only had his own rifle but had bagged a deer before.

Because his uncle was a little careless about routine matters, such as keeping food in the house, or doing laundry, Charlie had taken over most household duties and did most of the grocery shopping.

When Charlie told me how his uncle had sometimes failed to buy groceries, coming home with only a couple of six-packs, and I expressed criticism of a guardian who would let his ward go hungry, it was one of the few times Charlie got annoyed with me.

"Don't talk about my uncle. You don't know, he's a great man."

I changed the subject. After we had gotten to know each other well, I broached a subject I'd been curious about. "How come you live with your uncle instead of your mom and dad?"

At first, Charlie seemed reluctant to talk about his parents but then he told me his father had been in prison at Walla Walla for several years and he didn't know about his mother but he thought she might have died.

His father was in prison! I was duly impressed. "Do you ever go visit your dad in prison?"

"My uncle visits him sometimes and I asked him to take me along but he said he didn't think that would be a good idea."

There were a hundred questions I was dying to ask, but I knew I would be intruding where Charlie didn't welcome visitors. I left most of my questions unasked. I did work up the nerve to ask why Charlie's father was sent to prison.

"He killed a guy."

It was difficult to resist probing for details but I refrained. Charlie then added, without prompting, "My uncle told me the guy needed killing, but he didn't say how come."

Charlie was a more enthusiastic talker when the subject was hunting and his deer rifle. This aroused my serious envy. I was just hoping to get a BB gun for my 11th birthday in the summer. Charlie not only had his own rifle but it was a 30-30 Winchester lever action, the same rifle carried by comic book and matinee hero Red Ryder, my very most favorite hero.

I thought Red Ryder's faithful sidekick, an adopted Indian boy named Little Beaver, was the luckiest kid in the world. I wanted to share with my friend the wonderful world of Red Ryder's cattle ranch in Colorado and his adventures catching cattle rustlers, illegal miners and assorted other bad guys, stopping cattle stampedes at the last minute, at the edge of a cliff, and so on. I brought a couple of Red Ryder comic books to school to lend to Charlie. When Charlie returned them he laughed and said he thought they were kind of silly. "Sometimes," he said, "the white man is crazy."

Now it was my turn to be annoyed with Charlie, for the first and only time. Charlie sensed that he had offended me and sought to remedy the situation. He smiled, punched me playfully on the shoulder and said, "Naw, I'm just kidding. Red Ryder is okay."

I knew Charlie was lying, but I appreciated the words anyway. We talked no more about Red Ryder.

On a Spring day when we were sitting at noon hour in the bleachers beside the playfield (which was also the high school's football field), chatting about this and that, Charlie suddenly got a serious expression on his face and asked me if I could keep a secret.

"Sure. If you say it's a secret, I would never tell."

After a minute or so of silence -- I had learned to be patient waiting for

Charlie to speak -- Charlie said, "I'm going to tell you something I would never tell the white man, except you."

My curiosity surged.

"Talber is not really my name. That's just my name for the white man to know. My real name, my Indian name, is Tall Bear."

He studied my face. I realized what Charlie had just told me was more significant than I was able fully to understand. All I could think of to say was, "That's really neat. That's a great name. I like it." That was the truth. I rolled the name over and over in my mind, "Charlie Tall Bear, Charlie Tall Bear."

After another minute of silence, Charlie said, "I told you that so you can remember me by my real name. But don't tell anybody, OK?"

As I reaffirmed that I could be trusted with my friend's secret name I didn't immediately pick up on the implications of the reference to remembering him.

Charlie continued, "My uncle got a job with a guy he knows in Montana who runs rodeo stock. He's getting ready for rodeo season and he wants my uncle to come help him. We're leavin' for Montana this weekend."

I was stunned. In spite of knowing that Charlie had rarely been able to stay at a school for more than a few months at a time, the thought of my friend's departure had just never occurred to me. A moment later I was struck by another unhappy thought -- my protector's departure would leave me once more at the mercy of Dennis Wolfe, who would probably be meaner than ever now. And there was still almost a month of school to go.

At the supper table that evening, my mother looked unbelieving when I assured her I wasn't sick, as I picked at my food. She held the back of her hand to my forehead to check for a temperature. I forced down the food I really didn't want only because my stepfather didn't allow me to leave the table with anything left on my plate.

The next day was Friday and the day to say goodbye to Charlie.
During the first hour in class Charlie passed me a note. It was neatly printed -- a big improvement over his printing in December when I had started helping him.

I TOLD DENNIS WOLFE I AM COMING BACK TO TOWN BEFORE SCHOOL GETS OUT AND I WILL CHECK WITH YOU TO SEE IF HES PICKING ON YOU AGAIN. AND IF HE IS I WILL FIX HIM GOOD. I WONT REALLY BE BACK BUT HE THINKS SO.

I looked at Charlie, who was smiling. I put the note in my pocket.

At noon hour Charlie told me that if his warning to Dennis Wolfe didn't work, I should carry a rock in my pocket and use it on Dennis if he came close. I responded that I didn't think that was a good idea. If I really hurt Dennis with a rock, they might send me to reform school. Charlie smiled, shook his head slowly and said, "Sometimes the white man is just crazy."

Whether it was Charlie's warning or for some other reason, Dennis left me in peace the rest of the school term. There was one short letter from Charlie a few weeks after he left. I answered it but never heard from him again. I never forgot Charlie Tall Bear and I never revealed his true name to anyone.

The Dolan Place

Tom Dolan was getting on in years and his farm at the base of Whitestone Mountain required more work than he had energy for. So he sold a large piece of it to Mack and Lilly, including a small orchard of apples, pears and peaches, a hayfield and enough land for a large garden and livestock pens. What was not included was a house. We lived in an apartment in the Whitestone Hotel in town while Mack and Lilly, with the help of Ellen and me, built a large double garage with an attached woodshed and storeroom. We moved in with the intention of building a proper house beside the garage later. But the real house never materialized while we lived on the property.

The Dolan Place 1949

So, it was back to using an outhouse, with the Sears-Roebuck and Montgomery Ward (commonly called "Monkey Wards") catalogs for toilet paper (only the pages printed on uncoated paper were suitable for the purpose). Bathing was again done in a washtub with water heated on the wood-burning cook stove. Since there was no well, water for drinking and cooking had to be hauled out from town in large milk cans but flume water was usable for washing and laundry. A plus was the discovery of ice under the talus at the base of the mountain. Digging an ice cave provided a natural refrigerator for perishable foodstuffs.

Tending the orchard and hayfield and a huge garden, as well as chickens and pigs to feed, made plenty of work for everyone. My favorite thing about the Dolan Place was the "puddlejumper" our stepfather bought. Puddlejumpers were old trucks that had been cut down and modified for use as tractors. They were a common implement on small farms and orchards whose owners couldn't afford a Ferguson or Farmall or other proper tractor. Our puddlejumper had been a 1926 International truck. The cab had been removed, the wheelbase was shortened and extra large tires were mounted. A concrete slab was fitted above the axle to provide good traction. I loved to ride on the open air seat beside my stepfather as he plowed or disked or cut hay. Somewhat surprisingly, it was allowed.

This led to an incident that caused me to puzzle over my relationship with my stepfather. One day while newly plowed ground was being disked, I noticed a sizable rock on my side of the puddlejumper, in the path of the disking attachment being pulled along behind. I jumped off and lifted the rock out of the way as the disks rolled by. The puddlejumper stopped instantly and my stepfather swung around on the seat to look for me. After staring at me a few seconds he shouted, "What in hell are you doing?"

"Moving this rock so the disker won't hit it."

"Are you nuts? What if you tripped and fell in front of the disks? Get into the house and stay there."

I dropped the rock and trotted to the house. I was puzzled by my stepfather's reaction when he thought I was in danger. It wasn't the anger I was so accustomed to provoking in my stepfather. It was more like fear and concern.

When my stepfather came into the house a little later he told my mother he saw me, out of the corner of his eye, disappear off the puddlejumper and he thought I had fallen off. Fearing that I might be lying in the path of the disks, he slammed on the brakes. He was surprised to see me calmly picking up a rock as the disks churned the ground a few feet from me. Designed to slice through large clods of soil turned up by plowing, the disks would make short work of any person or animal they ran over.

I was sternly warned never again to get off the puddlejumper when it was moving and only with permission when it wasn't. And that was all. The expected punishment didn't happen. A few days later I was again allowed to ride on the puddlejumper.

Thinking about the incident later, I remembered another time when my stepfather's attitude toward me was uncharacteristically solicitous. The first Winter when we moved to Eastern Washington and were living in the stepuncle's house on the orchard, I came down sick and was in bed with fever and vomiting for several days. One evening, when I felt especially miserable and my fever was high, my stepfather came into the room and sat beside the bed. He talked about some of his experiences as a boy on the homestead at Alta Lake, being stalked by a cougar as he walked home one evening, and about trying his hand at panning for gold in California. He had never before told me anything about himself. He even told me that his name was really Dwight McKinley Sawyer but that he disliked the name Dwight so always went by the short version of his middle name. Only his mother and sisters called him Dwight. After a couple of fistfights when they were boys, he persuaded his brothers to call him Mack.

I had been too sick at the time to think about the "why" of my stepfather's actions. But later, after the sickness was in the past, I overheard my mother and stepfather talking and learned that my illness had been scarlet fever. I had heard of that and knew it was sometimes fatal to children. I was glad I hadn't known at the time that I had scarlet fever. I guessed my stepfather, and my mother, had thought I might be at death's door that evening.

I decided my stepfather's makeup might have more twists and turns than I had realized. It didn't make me feel closer to my stepfather, but it provoked some ambiguity.

While living at the Dolan Place, I had my first experience with free enterprise and consumerism. On Saturday and Sunday mornings, from Spring to Fall, I pulled my old Radio Flyer wagon along the road a mile or so North and then back South all the way into town. By the time I got to town I would have a few dozen beer bottles in the wagon that I'd picked up in the ditches beside the road where they'd been tossed from passing vehicles the night before.

Beer and soda in those years included a two-cent bottle deposit in the purchase price. Bringing those bottles back to the grocery store, I collected the two-cent refund on each. Two or three dozen beer bottles put what I considered serious money in my pocket. I always asked to be paid with all dimes and nickels instead of a quarter or fifty-cent piece. I liked the clink and jingle of several coins when I jiggled my pocket.

At that time the Saturday afternoon kids' matinee at the Tonasket movie house cost twelve cents admission. Popcorn was a dime and most candy bars were a nickel. My favorite, a Mounds bar, cost eight cents.

Inevitably, I realized that swiping bottles from those stacked behind the store was faster and easier than collecting them along the road. But my first foray into crime ended badly -- I got caught. That cut short my criminal career.

About this time I found myself entertaining thoughts that were confusing and troubling. In science class at school the students had been introduced to the wonders of the universe. The incredible numbers needed to describe the universe I found difficult to grasp and a little scary. The worst concept was that of an infinite universe. The idea of space going on forever, with no end, no edge, no boundary, stuck in my mind the way a song can get stuck and keep playing over and over. Many Fall evenings I lay in the yard, keeping my dog company, and staring up at the stars and trying to imagine that the light I was seeing had been traveling through space for millions or even billions of years.

Compounding this intellectual burden was my first exposure to organized religion. My sister Ellen became interested in the Free Methodist Church in town and, despite the vigorous discouragement of our mother and stepfather, began attending Sunday services. The church also had services on Saturday evening but Ellen couldn't get permission to attend those. Saturday nights traditionally belonged to parents. It was their night to go dancing at the Grange Hall or to some other event. Children were allowed to go to the movies or to ball games or school dances on Friday evenings but were expected to stay home while their parents enjoyed their Saturday night out.

Ellen decided she must find a way to attend the Saturday evening services. Her simple expedient was to wait until our mother and step- father had gone out and then go absent without leave, returning well before they would get home. She couldn't leave me home for two reasons. First, if she did, I might tell on her. Second, she wanted company on the three-mile walk into town in the dark and even more so on the walk home later. As we walked the road along the river we had to hide from the infrequent passing cars because they might contain people who would recognize us and report our unauthorized outing. Even worse, the headlights could be on the pickup truck that was at that time our family car.

Among the topics discussed at the Saturday evening services was eternal life for those who pass muster on the final day of this world. Most of the congregation seemed to find the idea of eternal life comforting. But I started trying to grasp the full meaning of eternity -- life without end, with no edge, no boundary, no final limit. The twin conundrums of infinity and eternity became personal demons that haunted me and began to drain the joy out of being alive. Sometimes I almost felt physically ill as they festered in my mind like infections. It required all my will to force them slowly into a nether recess of my consciousness where I could lock them away.

The Winter of '48

The Winter of 1948/49 was extra cold and snowy. Well before Christmas the wind blowing down the valley from Canada had become so raw that our stepfather, with my help, nailed large canvas tarps across the North wall of the garage/house. Unfortunately, that was the side with the only two windows. The tarps cut off the only source of natural light so that lamps had be kept on all day. Otherwise, the interior would be totally dark except for the reddish glow on the sides of the potbellied heating stove. Fires were kept going around the clock in both stoves but their heat could only be felt for a short distance. The water bucket that sat on the kitchen counter, not far from the cook stove, had a thin crust of ice in the morning that had to be broken before water could be dippered out.

Sawing and chopping wood had become another of my jobs. Even inside the woodshed, sheltered from the direct blast of the wind, I could only work for about a half-hour at a stretch before needing to go inside and put my feet near the potbellied stove to warm them up.

Sometimes they got so cold that when they began to warm up they would ache enough to bring tears and then they'd begin to itch like crazy. When I put my shoes and galoshes back on, my feet would sometimes be swollen, making it difficult to tie the laces.

I checked the thermometer in the woodshed every morning as I headed down to the road to wait for the school bus, often seeing a temperature South of 20 below. The one good thing about that winter was that it so demanded every bit of physical and mental endurance that philosophical concepts couldn't compete and I finally got eternity and infinity out of my head.

A little after this time I discovered the mental trick of getting my consciousness out of my head. One day, when some visitors were sitting around the table with our mother and stepfather, chatting over coffee, I was slouching in the big leather easy chair. If my stepfather had noticed me slouching he would have ordered me to sit up straight. Good posture, our stepfather believed, was an indicator of good character. I was engaged in not being heard, as was expected of children when adults were speaking. I didn't mind at all being out of the conversation because it held no interest for me. As I sat looking in the direction of the adults but not really seeing them, hearing their conversation as a kind of meaningless drone or chant, I had a peculiar sensation of my self-awareness floating out through my eyes and hovering in space, like a disembodied spirit. I felt disconnected from my body, as if some communications network had been shut down. There was a sense of unreality, as if I were dreaming. But I knew I was wide awake. The feeling was a little scary, so I forced myself to move my arms and legs, glad for the reassurance that I could reconnect my mental and physical states when I wanted to.

I thought about that experience a lot in the following days. I decided to try to induce the sensation again. The first few times I had no success. But I finally discovered the conditions around me had to be just right and I had to be in the right frame of mind.

After a while I quit bringing it on deliberately but it would still happen every now and then. I would quickly undertake physical movement to dissipate the sensation. It made me feel lonely when it happened. It made me strongly aware that each person is a thing unto himself or herself. Mothers and best buddies notwithstanding, everyone is basically alone in the world. Nobody can get born for you or do your dying for you, or do your striving or suffering. It made me fully realize, as I hadn't before, the implications of ceasing to exist some day. Knowing that every living thing must die had only been an abstraction before. I had never identified it with myself. I tried to remember when I had first become aware of death and recalled the time when our stepfather's stepfather had died on the sofa in our living room in the log house. Ellen and I didn't really know him but we cried a lot anyway.

It made the concepts of eternity and infinity seem less important.

The Hunt

When my mother awakened me, long before dawn, I hopped out of bed quickly, contrary to my usual reluctance to emerge from a warm bed into the cold autumn air. My feet barely felt the chill of the concrete floor through the thin throw rug. As I breathed deeply the cooking smells wafting through the house, I pulled on my longjohns, Frisco jeans, heavy wool socks and boots. I grabbed a flannel shirt and wool sweater and my mackinaw and hurried to the table where my mother was about to deliver a tall stack of hotcakes and a plate of sausage patties. Our stepfather was going deer hunting this Fall day in 1949 and I was going along for the first time.

Before leaving, I had chores to do, especially feeding the chickens, which would be butchered soon. In the Fall weather the grain for the chickens was soaked in water in a large keg behind the cook stove, where it maintained a warm temperature. I had to push the scoop all the way to the bottom of the keg and bring up grain that had been soaking for several days. It had begun to ferment and the smell that came up with it turned my stomach if I didn't hold my nose. When I had the right amount of the stinking mash in the bucket I poured an equal amount of dry grain into the keg.

I carried the bucket of mash and a bucket of water up the path in the frosty dark to the chicken coop. I emptied the mash into a long, shallow trough and then knocked the ice out of the water pans before pouring in warm water. By the time the chickens finished the mash and began drinking, the water would be cool. Within a half-hour the water would have a shell of ice. As the morning wore on, the ice would melt and then when night came, any remaining water would freeze again.

As I came back into the house, the phone rang. It was one long and two short rings, indicating the call was for us. It was only the second phone we'd ever had at home. We shared a "party line" with six or seven other homes. It was common for some people to pick up their receivers as soon as the phone stopped ringing so they could listen in on the conversation. Nobody ever said anything on a party line they didn't want to be widely known within hours. As more people listened in, the signal weakened until the talking parties had to almost shout in order to hear each other.

The phone conversation was brief. It was just Ray Pike confirming that he would be at Blackie's service station at 6:30.

After meeting Mr. Pike at Blackie's, we crossed the bridge into town and drove to Pine's Tourist Cabins overlooking the river. My stepfather's friend, Leo Thorsen, was ready to go when Mack tapped on his cabin door. I was squeezed between the two men in the cab of the pickup as we headed North toward Ellisford. Mr. Pike followed in his pickup. We crossed back over the river at Ellisford and continued North a few miles to a county road leading up into the Cascade foothills. In a little over 30 minutes we came to where the pavement ended, about 50 feet beyond the entrance to the big Vernon LaSalle ranch. From there on the county road was gravel. It was about 8 o'clock and full light when we pulled off the road into a clearing in the trees.

As the men drank some coffee from their thermoses it was decided that I would accompany Mr. Pike and Leo would go with Mack. Leo was a long-time friend of Mack's who had worked on Grand Coulee Dam with him and a couple of other construction sites since then. He'd driven over from the coast to go deer hunting with him.

As the sun began to climb above the mountains to the East, the four of us separated into two parties and set off in different directions. I followed Mr. Pike taking an ambitious route up a steep slope to a first ridge, then another and another, each higher than the last. As we got higher, a thin blanket of early snow covered the ground in places.

I hadn't expected to go with Mr. Pike and was a little tense. Ray Pike was three-quarters Indian, although his facial features were more an inheritance of his white grandfather than his Indian ancestors. In all other ways he displayed Indian characteristics. He was widely known and respected in the county, growing and selling hay and cutting, raking and baling hay on contract for small farmers. What concerned me was that Mr. Pike always had seemed somewhat severe in manner when I'd been with my stepfather as he and Mr. Pike had some dealings together. Indeed, Mr. Pike seemed a lot like Mack Sawyer, a no-nonsense type who had little patience or sympathy for weakness or mistakes. Small wonder, I thought, that my stepfather and Mr. Pike were friends.

I was determined to give Mr. Pike no reason to be critical of me or give a bad report to my stepfather. A couple of times as we hiked I started to say something but then caught myself. I watched carefully where I walked to avoid stepping on a fallen branch that might break with a loud snap under my weight. When Mr. Pike stopped to scan the ground for deer sign, I stopped in my tracks and remained motionless until my companion moved again.

By mid-morning we had climbed quite a way up, to where there was more snow on the ground. The sun had become fairly intense, turning the snow to slush, requiring extra care to avoid slipping. The sun also made me unbutton my mackinaw and wish I had left my sweater in the pickup.

Finally, we spotted some deer droppings that appeared to be fresh that day. Mr. Pike changed direction and moved along a ridge line, being careful not to let himself become silhouetted. Late in the morning we came to a large open sloping meadow in a hollow between wooded ridges. Mr. Pike stopped where he could see most of the meadow. After a few minutes he squatted down, as if waiting for something. I was grateful for a chance to rest. Inside my mackinaw my undershirt and flannel shirt were damp with sweat. It puzzled me that in Fall it could be so warm during the day and so cold as soon as the sun went down. I moved behind a tree where I was well hidden from the meadow and pulled off my mackinaw and sweater, tying the sweater around my waist.

Slowly I moved closer to Mr. Pike and squatted down, a little behind and to one side. There was nothing handy to sit on. My eyes shifted from the meadow, where I could see no movement, to Mr. Pike, studying his profile for any sign that he was seeing something. Mr. Pike's face was impassive and his body was still.

I couldn't keep my thoughts from wandering. I imagined Mr. Pike in buckskins and war bonnet, like the Indians who rode in the rodeo parade in town. He would be an impressive figure mounted on an Apaloosa, in full regalia. He wasn't an overly large man, just under six feet and more wiry than husky. But he had a commanding presence. You knew to look at him he wasn't to be trifled with. My thoughts also went to my friend, Charlie Tall Bear, wondering where he was and whether he was in school and how he was doing. I was snapped back from mental wandering by Mr. Pike's very low but clear words.

"You hear that?"

I strained to hear something besides the soft rustle of the breeze in the branches overhead. I very much wanted to hear something significant, I didn't want to appear useless to have along. Just as I began to whisper a lie, "Yeah," I did hear something. It was a faint crackling of something moving through the quakenasp in the draw at the top of the meadow.

Mr. Pike slowly shifted to one knee and held his rifle where he could rapidly bring it to his shoulder. There was no further sound for a few minutes. I stared as hard as I could at the mouth of the draw, as if I could will a nice buck to appear. When I sensed a slight shift in Mr. Pike's position, I looked even harder and was thrilled to see what at any other time I would have missed, the head of a deer above a large bush. It was a doe, but there might be a buck or two somewhere in the draw. The doe moved slowly out into the meadow and began to graze on a small bush. In a few seconds another doe appeared. Little by little, several deer emerged from the draw, including a large buck with six points on each antler. There was also a four-point buck and a spike. The two bucks that could legally be taken were in the middle of the does where it was impossible to get a shot at them without the risk of hitting a doe. Some years the state fish and game department authorized a doe hunt, as a means of controlling the deer population. But this season they were protected.

I could feel the sun hot on the back of my neck and my legs were starting to ache from squatting so long. I marveled at Mr. Pike's seeming indifference to discomfort, especially for a man who had to be over 60 years old.

After an interval that seemed to me as if it would never end, the constant slow movements of the deer as they grazed, working their way down the meadow, finally exposed the four-point buck.

Mr. Pike brought his rifle to his shoulder, quickly lined his sights and sent a loud shaft of sound across the meadow. I couldn't keep myself from flinching. Before the sound would have reached the deer, the four-point jumped back a step, then forward to try to run, but his forelegs buckled and he crumpled to the ground. The rest of the deer stood motionless for one beat and then bounded back up the meadow into the draw. The sound of quakenasp branches snapping traced the movement of the deer up the draw until it was finally quiet again.

Mr. Pike remained in the same posture for a couple minutes, rifle at the ready, in case the buck was only wounded and could recover enough to get up and run. A hunter who wounded an animal was obliged to follow the animal, no matter how far, and finish it off. Of course, some hunters didn't bother. It was not that rare to find a deer carcass beginning to rot in a thicket where the coyotes, bobcats or cougars hadn't yet discovered it. Sometimes the bullet hole could be seen, in a haunch or another spot where it wouldn't kill immediately. But Mr. Pike was not such a hunter. He wanted to be sure he didn't have to trail a wounded deer.

Finally, Mr. Pike got to his feet and started down the slope, keeping his eyes on the downed buck. When we reached it we could see the bullet entry point at the base of the throat. The bullet had penetrated to the heart and brought almost instant death. Mr. Pike was known for routinely making shots like that.

He fastened his deer tag around an antler and slit the buck's throat. He turned the body with the head downhill to facilitate draining the blood, which was better for the quality of the meat.

We sat on a downed tree at the edge of the meadow and ate our sandwiches. After eating, Mr. Pike lit a cigarette and smoked it slowly, seemingly lost in thought. I was surprised when Mr. Pike began to talk. He asked about school and whether I liked to fish. When I said I did, Mr. Pike told me about a great fishing stream that not many people visited because it required a long hike. Then, even more surprisingly, he talked about how he had hunted with his father on the Colville Indian Reservation when he was a boy. He said his father could smell a deer a mile away. I was pretty sure he was kidding but couldn't tell by his expression.

After he carefully ground out his cigarette butt, he cut a sapling for a pole to sling the deer on for carrying it. He took the front end of the pole and I took the other end and we set off with the pole on our shoulders.

Hiking down with our burden was harder and slower than the hike up had been, but at least it was in more of a straight line. In an hour, my shoulder was aching but I didn't want to ask for a rest. To my immense relief, Mr. Pike stopped in a shady stand of trees and said, "Let's take a break."

After resting for about 15 minutes we set out again. In less than an hour we crested the ridge overlooking the clearing where the pickups were parked. Since there was no sign of Mack or Leo at the clearing, Mr. Pike called for another break. He sat on the ground with his back against a tree and lit up a cigarette. I noticed that he now looked tired. It gave me an unexpected sense of satisfaction. It was the first sign I'd seen that Mr. Pike was only human after all. I felt better about my own fatigue. Finishing his cigarette and carefully snubbing it out, Mr. Pike slowly rose to his feet, stretching and flexing with little grunting noises. He said, more to himself than to me, "I think I'm getting old," and took up his load again.

It didn't take long to get down from the ridge to the pickups. We deposited the buck in the bed of Mr. Pike's pickup. He emptied the shells from his rifle and put it away in its case behind the seat. Then he stretched out on the seat, with the passenger door open, and in a few minutes I could hear him snoring. Somehow, knowing Mr. Pike was bushed inspired me to deny my own aching muscles and leaden arms and legs. I got behind the wheel of my stepfather's pickup and pretended I was driving a race car in the Indy 500.

It was almost another hour before my stepfather and Leo came into view. They weren't carrying a deer. The sound of voices awakened Mr. Pike and I was surprised to see that an hour's nap seemed to have completely refreshed him. There was no sign of his earlier fatigue. My stepfather described the route he and Leo had followed and complained they saw some deer sign but not even a glimpse of a deer. My stepfather said, "I was up here two weeks ago and I saw at least a dozen right from the road. They were all over this area."

Mr. Pike responded, "Yeah, they seem to know when hunting season starts and when to make themselves scarce. The boy and I had to go way to hell and gone up above to find some."

I was pleased to hear him say, "The boy and I." It made me feel I had been a full partner in the hunt. My stepfather glanced at me and then toward Mr. Pike. "How'd the boy do? Was he any help?" I felt a twinge of apprehension waiting for the answer.

"Yeah, he did okay. He's a good hunter."

Mr. Pike looked toward me and actually smiled. It was only a faint smile that lasted just a few seconds, but I couldn't remember ever seeing him smile before. I felt like I got three inches taller at that moment. I had been pronounced satisfactory by a very stern judge. But if I hoped for some acknowledgement from my stepfather of Mr. Pike's approval, that hope faded quickly.

After a brief examination of Mr. Pike's buck, we all headed for home. Mr. Pike was first onto the road so my stepfather drove slowly at first to let the dust thrown up by the other pickup dissipate.

As we continued homeward, I felt a sense of satisfaction. The sun dipped below the Cascade peaks and a rosy twilight soon settled over the landscape. My stepfather and Leo were going hunting again the next day, trying their luck in a different area. I wouldn't be going with them because I would be in school.

I knew I wasn't yet a man but, for the first time, I felt I was no longer just a boy. I decided I was ready to start becoming a grown-up.

It was just full dark and getting cold as we pulled up the driveway next to the house. I jumped from the pickup before my stepfather would have a chance to tell me to get busy doing my chores. As I scooped some stinking mash into the bucket I said over my shoulder to my mother, in what I hoped was a nonchalant, matter-of-fact way, "Mr. Pike says I'm a good hunter."

The end.

About the Author

I was born in Seattle but mostly grew up in rural Eastern Washington. After graduation from Quincy High School in 1956 I joined the Navy and spent the next nineteen years "seeing the world," as they used to say in Navy recruiting literature and "seeing the U.S.A.," as they used to say in Chevrolet advertising. Along the way I acquired a wife in Boston and two children born in Illinois, one in Texas and another in Hawaii. My wife of 42 years died in 2004.

After retiring from the Navy in 1975 as a Master Chief Petty Officer, I returned with my family to Seattle and completed my BA at the University of Washington, graduating in 1977. I then went to work for SAFECO Insurance Company, from which I retired in 1999. Since then, I have worked as a volunteer for various non-profit organizations.

Over the years I have returned to Eastern Washington many times, to visit my mother and other relatives. It has very many memories for me, a few not so good but most of a positive nature. I realize how much the land East of the mountains influenced the person I became as an adult. Of course, it is no longer the same as when I grew up there.

This story is based on a memoir written for my children, grandchildren and those whose ancestor I will one day be. I wanted to give them a few snapshots of life in an earlier time and different environment than they are or will be familiar with. It is slightly fictionalized in some small details because there are some gaps in my early childhood memories.

At my website, woodyswords.com ,there are some Navy memoirs and a link to Woody's Classic Movie Reviews.

Made in the USA
San Bernardino, CA
20 June 2017